UNCOVERING HISTORY

MEDIEVAL EUROPE

Everyday Life in Medieval Europe
was created and produced by McRae Books Srl
Borgo Santa Croce, 8 – 50122 – Florence (Italy)
info@mcraebooks.com
www.mcraebooks.com

ISBN 88-89272-57-0

SERIES EDITOR Anne McRae
TEXT Neil Grant
ILLUSTRATIONS Manuela Cappon, Luisa Della Porta, Paola Ravaglia,
Andrea Ricciardi di Gaudesi, Studio Stalio (Alessandro Cantucci,
Fabiano Fabbrucci, Andrea Morandi)
GRAPHIC DESIGN Marco Nardi
LAYOUT Laura Ottina, Adriano Nardi
EDITING Susan Kelly and Vicky Egan
REPRO Litocolor, Florence
PICTURE RESEARCH Susan Kelly

Printed and bound in Italy

UNCOVERING HISTORY

Neil Grant

MEDIEVAL
EVERYDAY LIFE IN
EUROPE

Illustrations by Manuela Cappon, Luisa Della Porta, Paola Ravaglia, Andrea Ricciardi di Gaudesi, Studio Stalio

MCRAE BOOKS

Table of Contents

Introduction

The Medieval period, or the Middle Ages, covers about 1,000 years of European history, from the collapse of the Roman Empire in the 5th century to the Renaissance in the 15th century. During the early Middle Ages, the people of Europe lived in tribal groups led by kings, who were little more than warlords. But by 1500, a number of states had formed, some of which (England, France and Spain, for example) still have much the same boundaries today. Slowly, the population increased and forests and swamps were turned into farmland. The speed of change increased between 1000 and 1500 — the High Middle Ages — and this is the period of special interest to us. During this time, most people were poor peasants who worked the land. They could not read or write, and knew little of life outside their own villages. They were governed by two powerful institutions — the nobility and the Roman Catholic Church. The nobles were basically a class of warriors who controlled an area of land and its people. The peasants served the nobility. The Church, led by the pope, also demanded obedience from the people. Practically everyone believed in the Christian God, and they also believed that the Church alone knew what God wanted. From about the 13th century, the nobility were challenged by the growing power of the kings and the rich merchants in towns. The Church became divided, the pope lost influence and critics of the Church spoke out and demanded changes. The weakening power of the Church and nobility, and the gradual development of a new kind of society, led to the end of the Middle Ages.

ABBOT BENEDICT ESTABLISHES HIS
RULE FOR MONASTERIES
about 525

CHARLEMAGNE CROWNED HOLY
ROMAN EMPEROR BY THE POPE
800

ONE OF THE FIRST UNIVERSITIES IS
FOUNDED IN BOLOGNA, ITALY
about 1088

FIRST CRUSADE LAUNCHED AGAINST
MUSLIMS IN PALESTINE
1096

THE HANSEATIC LEAGUE
(OF TRADING CITIES IN NORTHERN
EUROPE) IS FOUNDED
1241

THE BLACK DEATH REACHES EUROPE
1348

THE GREAT SCHISM,
WITH TWO RIVAL POPES,
DIVIDES THE CHRISTIAN CHURCH
1378–1417

THE OTTOMAN TURKS
CONQUER SOUTHEASTERN EUROPE
1389

THE FIRST PRINTED BOOK
IS PUBLISHED
1455

THE LAST MUSLIM STATE
IS CONQUERED BY THE SPANIARDS
1492

Society

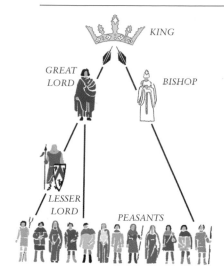

The population can be seen as a pyramid, with the peasants at the bottom forming about 90 percent of the total. Above them in rank were the nobility and lesser landowners. Higher still came the Church — bishops ranked equally with the great lords. At the top is the king, who not only held the largest estates but, in theory, owned the whole kingdom.

People in medieval Europe belonged to one of three main groups: those who fought (the nobles); those who prayed (the Church); and those who worked (the peasants, who were the huge majority). The nobles ruled large estates, and the peasants worked for them. In a sense, the whole kingdom belonged to the king, who gave land to great lords in return for their loyalty and military service. The great lords gave land to lesser lords and knights, in return for their service, and so on. People stayed all their lives in the class they were born into. To rise higher in the social scale was regarded as a sin, and to fall lower was thought shameful. But by the 14th century, these attitudes were beginning to change. Towns were growing, and for the first time people were working for wages — paid in money — rather than goods. Gradually, this weakened the bonds between servant and master.

Small worlds

Most people lived in a very small world that extended no farther than their lord's lands. They had little idea of a 'nation', and did not think of themselves as 'English' or 'French', for example. Knights saw themselves not as a subject of the king, but as 'Lord So-and-so's man'. The central government, as represented by the king, had much less influence on people's lives than governments of today.

Peasants worked in the shadow of their lord's castle. They might live their whole lives in the same place, never venturing more than a few miles from where they were born.

During the Middle Ages, a king could not rule without the support of his lords. Often he had to assert his power over them, if they acted independently or tried to rebel against him. Royal ceremonies, such as this wedding, were conducted by bishops, which gave the monarchy an air of religious mystery.

Knights

Knights were a kind of junior nobility. Their first duty was to fight for their lord on powerful warhorses. Many were the younger sons of nobles, and were not in line to inherit estates. But by the later Middle Ages, knights usually had land of their own. During the Crusades, religious 'orders' of knights, such as the Knights Templars, were founded to fight for Christian lands in the Holy Land. Later, non-religious orders were also formed, such as the Knights of the Garter in England (1349).

The son of a knight trained to be a knight himself by serving another knight. When his lord decided he was ready, he knighted the young man by tapping his shoulders with a sword.

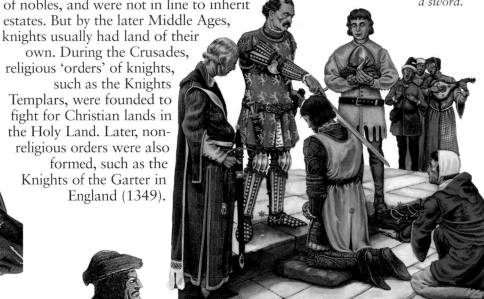

Chivalry

Knights were supposed to follow certain rules of behavior — the ideals of chivalry. They had a duty to be brave and honourable, loyal to God and their lord, generous even to their enemies, kind to the sick and the poor and gallant to women. Such ideals inspired the knightly orders, and were common themes in stories (for example those about King Arthur and his knights). But in reality, most knights fell short of these high standards.

A lord, on his knees, swears an oath of loyalty to the king. This made him a vassal of the king. Even the greatest lords were his vassals. They, in turn, had vassals who had sworn an oath to serve them, in exchange for land; these lesser lords had vassals of their own, and so on.

Vassals and land

Society was structured on the idea that a person gave his support to someone else in return for a grant of land. Anyone who received land in this way was called a vassal. A man's wealth and importance was measured by the amount of land he owned. The main cause of wars between kings or rival nobles was their desire for more land.

Serfs

A lord's land had value because it was worked by peasants and serfs. In some places, a man's wealth was measured not in acres, but by the number of serfs he owned. Serfs were not slaves, but neither were they free. They usually worked for their lords for several days a week, and were forbidden to move to another village, or to marry, without the permission of their lord. It was rare for farms to be held by free men who were not bound to a landlord.

Loyalty and protection

Although serfs were like slaves in that they had to obey their lord — and he could sell or give them away — the lord also had a duty to protect them and to settle their disputes justly in his court. This duty depended on custom, not on a legal document, and not all lords treated their serfs fairly. Serfdom had almost disappeared in western Europe by 1500, but it continued in Russia until 1861.

Both serfs and free peasants lived in basic conditions. They often shared their simple homes with their animals. The landlords lived in far greater comfort, supported by a large household. The peasants provided food for the household.

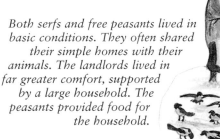

The Christian Church

The greatest power in medieval Europe was the Church, headed by the pope in Rome. Kings and lords ruled men's bodies, but the Church ruled their souls. This was a useful partnership. Rulers needed the Church, representing God, to support their authority. In return, they gave the Church protection. The Church was rich, and its influence was huge. Few people disagreed with its teachings, at least not openly. Those who did were punished as 'heretics'. Ultimately, people feared that if they seriously disobeyed the Church, they would go to Hell when they died. Still, many people criticized the behaviour of priests, and a few challenged the pope's authority. Some of the popes and kings argued about the legal position of bishops and priests: to whom was their first loyalty due — the king or the pope?

This crucifix dates from the time of King Ferdinand the Great of Castile and Leon (died 1065), who began the Christian crusade to drive the Muslims out of Spain.

The bishop of Rome — the pope — claimed power over all Christians in western Europe.

The clergy

There were huge numbers of clergy, of different ranks. Below the pope came the bishops, then parish priests, and below them humble clerks, some of whom were hardly educated. All of these were secular clergy — they were not bound by a religious rule. Clergy who belonged to religious orders included monks and friars. Abbots and bishops had great power, and some were effectively local princes.

The pope

This 12th-century drawing (left) shows Pope Gregory VII (1073–85), one of the greatest medieval popes, excommunicating a king. Excommunication meant expulsion from the Church, and was disastrous for a ruler. The long off-and-on conflict between popes and rulers over the divided loyalties of the clergy began when Gregory attempted, with partial success, to unite Christian Europe under papal leadership.

Art and the Church

Some of the finest creations in all European art are the cathedrals, churches and abbeys of the Middle Ages. They are a testament to the strong religious faith of the people. In the Gothic period (the 12th to 15th centuries), church roofs and spires were built higher and higher, reflecting a desire to be closer to God (as well as an ambition to build a finer church than the neighbouring town's!). Most art was religious, and was done to help people worship God.

The Church taught that life on Earth was a painful preparation for eternal life in Heaven. Heretics — people who disagreed with the Church's teachings — were tortured or killed.

Relics

Every church and abbey hoped to own a relic, such as the body, or even just a bone, of a Christian saint. Holy relics were believed to have special healing powers, and pilgrims travelled great distances, and gave the Church money, to see them. Many relics were not genuine.

Saints' relics were kept in special containers called reliquaries, some of which were very valuable. They were often made by the finest medieval goldsmiths.

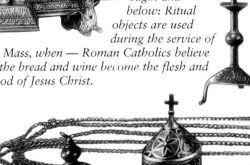

Roman Catholics continue to worship the Virgin Mary — the mother of Jesus — with devotion.

Corruption and division

The Church was often accused of greed, dishonesty and corruption by people who wanted to reform its ways. Some priests and monks were worse sinners than the people they preached to, and many bishops and popes were more interested in increasing their own wealth than in performing their religious duties. From 1378 to 1417, the papacy was weakened in the Great Schism, when there were two rival popes (one in Rome, one in Avignon).

Right and below: Ritual objects are used during the service of the Mass, when — Roman Catholics believe — the bread and wine become the flesh and blood of Jesus Christ.

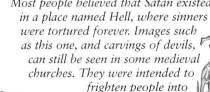

This chalice was used in the Orthodox Church, the religion of the Byzantine (or Eastern Roman) Empire, which included parts of southeastern Europe. There were few contacts between the Orthodox and Roman Catholic Churches, despite their many similarities.

Most people believed that Satan existed in a place named Hell, where sinners were tortured forever. Images such as this one, and carvings of devils, can still be seen in some medieval churches. They were intended to frighten people into good behaviour.

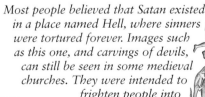

When a person is baptized, he is anointed with holy water from a font, such as this one from the 12th century. It was customary, as it still is in many churches, to baptize children soon after they were born. Through baptism, Christians believe, a person becomes a full member of the Church.

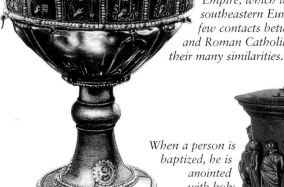

Churches

The loudest noise in the countryside of Christian Europe was the sound of church bells. The church was the centre of village life. Everyone had to attend church services, even though they were held in Latin, which few people understood. With the exception of Jews, no one was allowed to follow a form of Christianity not approved by the pope, or be a non-believer.

Government

In the days of the Roman Empire, all Europe was ruled by the same government, and there was one set of laws. But after the fall of Rome, the system of government and justice collapsed. Every lord in his castle was able to behave much as he pleased. Personal bonds between masters and servants developed as a way of providing security during these dangerous times. Gradually, central government and the rule of law were slowly restored as royal powers increased. The king was everyone's overlord. The Church supported royal government because it promised law and order. And the Church represented the one absolute authority that everyone recognized — God.

Trial by ordeal

Many people accused of crimes had to prove their innocence or guilt by undergoing a 'trial by ordeal', such as gripping a red-hot iron. If the scars healed, they were innocent; if they did not heal, they were guilty, and probably died from their wounds. Intelligent people disapproved of trials by ordeal, and in 1215 the Church banned them from their courts. In the later period, in the English royal courts, juries decided whether an accused person was guilty or innocent. In other countries, judges gave the verdict.

Punishment

Medieval punishments were harsh and cruel. In local courts, people who had committed small offenses were either fined or put in the stocks — a wooden frame with foot holes, in which offenders were locked — so that passers-by could throw rotten vegetables at them. More serious offenses were punished by beatings, branding or cutting off a hand or ear. Torture was sometimes also used to make a prisoner confess first. Several crimes carried the death penalty.

Royal income

Kings gained an income from their estates and various other dues, but it was seldom enough to cover their needs. In times of war — always an expensive business — they had to raise huge additional sums, which they often did by imposing new taxes. Customs duties from trade were another useful source of income for rulers.

Rebellious lords often challenged the power of the king. In 1215, when King John of England signed the Great Charter (Magna Carta), he agreed to uphold the rights of his subjects, and abide by the laws of England, just like everybody else. Some sections of the Charter are still part of English law today.

King and council

In England, the royal court was the centre of both government and justice, but the king was not an absolute ruler whose word was law. He governed with the advice of the royal council, made up of leading nobles and bishops. But government and justice were still handled mostly by local people in their own districts. The royal council sometimes did not meet for months.

Parliament

In order to govern well and, in particular, to raise taxes, the royal council needed information about local conditions throughout the kingdom. So it summoned local representatives from the towns and explained to them why various taxes had to be raised, especially in times of war, in the hope that this would make people more willing to pay. In England, these meetings developed into a parliament, which centuries later replaced the king as the supreme government. In France, the *parlements* developed in the same way, though they became courts rather than law-making bodies.

Simon de Montfort (left) led a successful revolt by English barons demanding the reform of royal government. In 1265, he called a parliament that included knights and men from the towns, but he was killed a few months later.

In 1295, England's King Edward I ordered two knights from each county and two representatives from each town to attend parliament, in addition to the nobles and churchmen. This assembly was the beginning of the British House of Commons.

City governments

As towns expanded and grew rich, the chief citizens sometimes managed to gain power from local lords. With the monarch as their overlord, cities had greater control of their own affairs, especially in the Holy Roman Empire (mainly Germany and Italy) and other countries where the ruler was weak or away from home. Some cities became 'communes', with a large degree of independence guaranteed by charter. A few even became republics. But their governments were usually quickly overthrown by other small groups of people hungry for power.

Like many Italian cities, the city of Perugia, pictured here protected by the hands of its patron saint, was a commune. Its overlord was the pope, but it was independent and self-governing. In the 15th century, however, the Baglioni family gained control.

Food and Farming

This man is harvesting grain with a one-handed sickle. Holding a bunch of stalks in one hand, he cuts them with the other.

Crops

The main food crops were cereals such as wheat and rye, as well as oats and barley in the north. Vegetables such as beans and peas were quite widely grown, and hay was made to feed the animals. Other vegetables and fruit were grown on a much smaller scale. Medieval farmers practiced a three-year crop rotation system (perhaps rye, followed by beans and then hay). They gained more farmland by draining marshes and felling forests.

About 80 percent of people worked on the land, and even townspeople grew vegetables and kept chickens, a pig and often a cow. People grew nearly all their own food and depended on a good harvest to get them through the winter. If the harvest failed, they died of starvation. It was difficult to import food from other regions, and famines happened about once every ten years. In most of Europe, the local village or manor belonged to a lord and was managed by his steward. Peasants worked on the estate in exchange for land they could farm for themselves. They also gave their lord a share of their own produce. By the 15th century, most peasants in western Europe worked for wages and paid rent for their land.

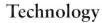

Olives were a vital crop in the south; some farmers grew nothing else. Olives provided oil, not only for cooking, but also for burning in lamps such as this one. In a few places, walnuts were used for the same purpose.

Technology

Medieval people used machines and developed new techniques to harness natural forces. Most villages had a mill for grinding grain into flour. (Water mills date from Roman times, and windmills appeared in the 12th century.) Peasants used plows drawn by oxen or horses, which was very hard work. The invention of the mold-board, which broke up the surface as well as turned the soil over, made the task of plowing much easier.

The Crusaders saw windmills in the Holy Land and brought the idea back with them. In Europe, where the winds are more changeable, post mills were used: the body of the mill turned, so that the sails could face the direction of the wind.

Diet

The staple food was bread made from rye or wheat. It was dark, coarse and gritty. White bread made from wheat was rare and was a sign of high social status. Most people ate few vegetables and little fruit, and they believed that greens were dangerous. Wine and olive oil were staples in southern Europe; beer and butter were common in the north.

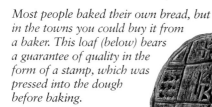

Most people baked their own bread, but in the towns you could buy it from a baker. This loaf (below) bears a guarantee of quality in the form of a stamp, which was pressed into the dough before baking.

Right: Sugar was unknown in most of Europe during the Middle Ages. The main sweetener was honey. This beekeeper is using smoke to drive away the bees while he collects their honey.

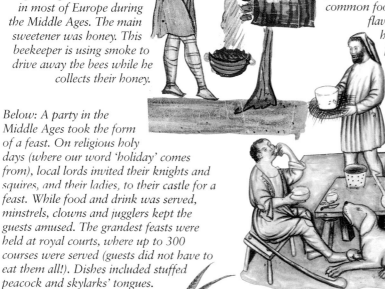

Because few crops were grown (there were almost no root vegetables), meals were monotonous, especially for the poor. Besides bread, the most common food for peasants was soup flavoured with bones and herbs. They also ate forest fruits and nuts, soup made from nettles, and, in an emergency, bread made from acorns.

Below: A party in the Middle Ages took the form of a feast. On religious holy days (where our word 'holiday' comes from), local lords invited their knights and squires, and their ladies, to their castle for a feast. While food and drink was served, minstrels, clowns and jugglers kept the guests amused. The grandest feasts were held at royal courts, where up to 300 courses were served (guests did not have to eat them all!). Dishes included stuffed peacock and skylarks' tongues.

Animals

For most people, meat was a luxury. One lean, bristly pig might have to last a family all winter. But pigs were easy to feed and often foraged for themselves in the forests (above). The most common farm animals were probably sheep, which were bred for wool as well as meat. (Europe had more sheep than people.) Cattle and chickens were also kept, and peasants were allowed to catch the odd rabbit or crow, or smaller birds. The rich, in contrast, had plenty of meat, including venison and other wild game. Hunting rights were reserved for the great landowners.

A Merchant's Home

Although Europe today is dotted with the ruins of medieval castles, the homes of ordinary people have mostly disappeared. Peasants' cottages were no more than shacks. Dark, damp and dirty, they were built of the cheapest materials available and often lasted less than a lifetime. Towns were small at first, and the houses like those in the villages. But as towns grew, houses were built taller and closer together. They often had an overhanging upper story, and in the narrow streets there was no room for kitchen gardens. A house might be shared by several families, each living in a single room. Fire was a constant danger, and houses often burned down before they fell down. The more successful merchants and businessmen, and even some craftsmen, were able to afford larger, more comfortable town houses, which can still be seen in the old quarters of many European towns.

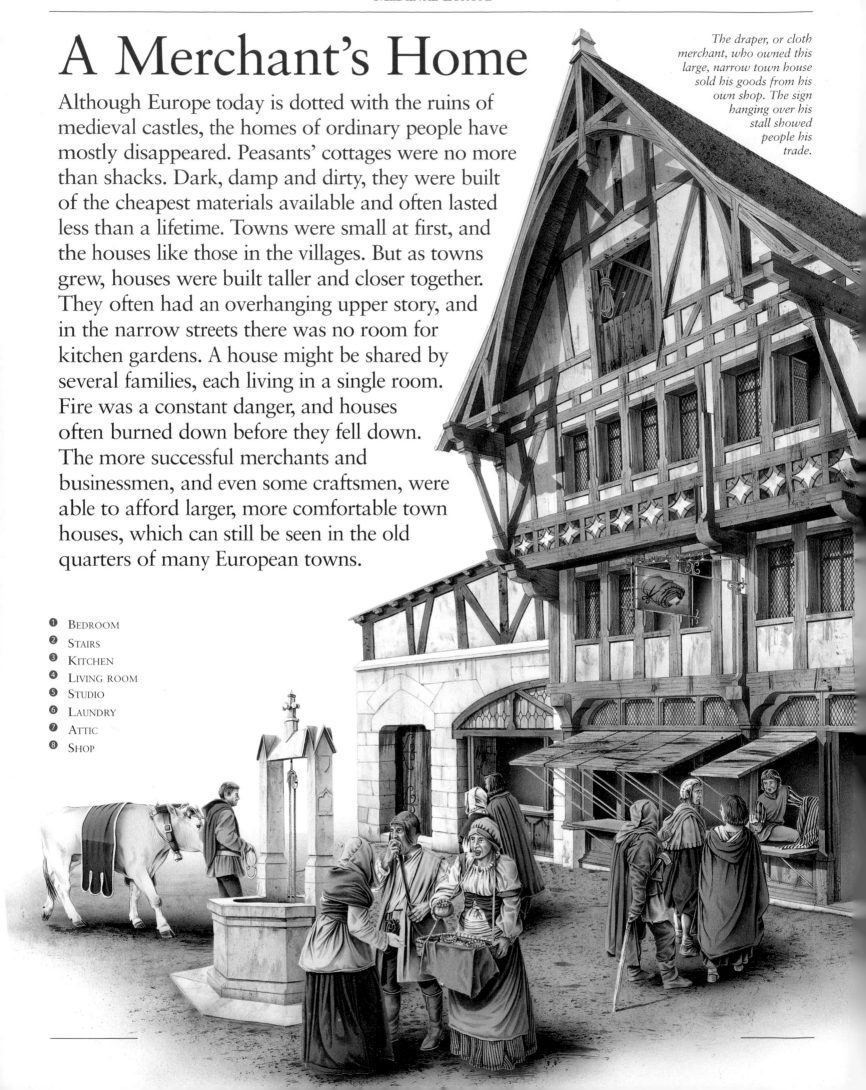

The draper, or cloth merchant, who owned this large, narrow town house sold his goods from his own shop. The sign hanging over his stall showed people his trade.

1 BEDROOM
2 STAIRS
3 KITCHEN
4 LIVING ROOM
5 STUDIO
6 LAUNDRY
7 ATTIC
8 SHOP

In a well-to-do merchant's house, you might see objects from all over Europe. This hand-painted cup and jug, for instance, were made in Orvieto, Italy, but the cup was found in an English house.

Home and workplace

The home of a merchant or businessman was also his office and even 'factory'. In the house of Jean Boine Broke, a rich Flemish draper in Douai, for example, cloth was not only sold, but was also made — from raw wool to finished material. Houses had to be secure against mobs or robbers, and lower windows were barred and shuttered (glass windows were unusual before the 15th century). The rest of the house was home for the merchant, his wife, their children and probably other relatives, as well as his apprentices and servants.

The new rich

In the late Middle Ages, it became easier for a man from a poor home to become wealthy through his own efforts, usually in trade. A wealthy merchant with a fine town house would usually invest his profits in land. Once he became a landowner, his descendants might join the nobility.

This rare closet from the 12th century is strong and simple, with just a little decoration on the side panels and fine iron hinges and locks. It was used to store linen and clothes.

Furnishings

Medieval houses had surprisingly little furniture, especially fine pieces. People sat on stools or benches rather than chairs, and coffers or plain chests were used for storage. The most valuable piece of furniture was the bed. Beds were usually large (one English bed was 14 feet [3.4 m] wide). In poorer houses, the whole family slept in one bed. Rich people often had beautiful tapestries on the walls and around their beds, which helped keep out drafts, but most of the furniture was fairly plain.

This large jar was probably used for storing food. Only fairly rich families could afford decorated pottery. The very rich owned silver vessels.

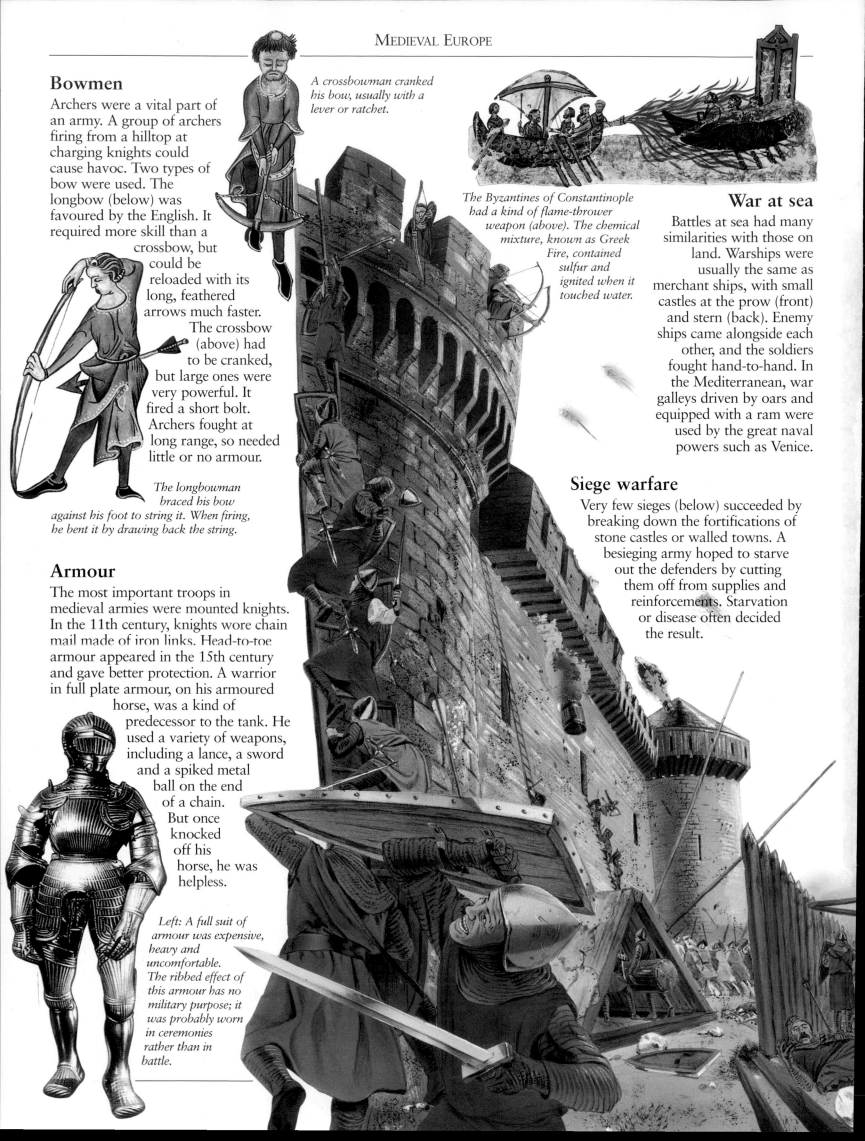

Bowmen

Archers were a vital part of an army. A group of archers firing from a hilltop at charging knights could cause havoc. Two types of bow were used. The longbow (below) was favoured by the English. It required more skill than a crossbow, but could be reloaded with its long, feathered arrows much faster. The crossbow (above) had to be cranked, but large ones were very powerful. It fired a short bolt. Archers fought at long range, so needed little or no armour.

The longbowman braced his bow against his foot to string it. When firing, he bent it by drawing back the string.

A crossbowman cranked his bow, usually with a lever or ratchet.

The Byzantines of Constantinople had a kind of flame-thrower weapon (above). The chemical mixture, known as Greek Fire, contained sulfur and ignited when it touched water.

War at sea

Battles at sea had many similarities with those on land. Warships were usually the same as merchant ships, with small castles at the prow (front) and stern (back). Enemy ships came alongside each other, and the soldiers fought hand-to-hand. In the Mediterranean, war galleys driven by oars and equipped with a ram were used by the great naval powers such as Venice.

Siege warfare

Very few sieges (below) succeeded by breaking down the fortifications of stone castles or walled towns. A besieging army hoped to starve out the defenders by cutting them off from supplies and reinforcements. Starvation or disease often decided the result.

Armour

The most important troops in medieval armies were mounted knights. In the 11th century, knights wore chain mail made of iron links. Head-to-toe armour appeared in the 15th century and gave better protection. A warrior in full plate armour, on his armoured horse, was a kind of predecessor to the tank. He used a variety of weapons, including a lance, a sword and a spiked metal ball on the end of a chain. But once knocked off his horse, he was helpless.

Left: A full suit of armour was expensive, heavy and uncomfortable. The ribbed effect of this armour has no military purpose; it was probably worn in ceremonies rather than in battle.

War

After the fall of the Roman Empire, when the future European nations were tribes, they were led by warlords and warriors. During the Middle Ages, kings and nobles had the same status — they were a military elite. The king was a warlord, and the chief duty of the nobles was to fight. Warfare was almost the normal state of things. During the Hundred Years' War, much of France never knew more than a few years of peace. Even when there was no war, gangs of mercenaries (men who fought for anyone who would pay them) roamed the land making trouble. But battles were sometimes less bloody than you might expect. Soldiers often fought to capture rather than kill, so they could demand a ransom. Sieges were more common than battles. An invading army could not afford to leave fortified towns untaken.

By the 15th century, most galleys were equipped with cannons. This strange vessel is packed with soldiers, showing that hand-to-hand fighting is expected.

War machines

For a thousand years, siege machines changed little. They included battering rams, giant catapults and towers on wheels that allowed the soldiers inside to get alongside a town's walls. From about 1320, cannons were used along with traditional war machines. The attackers now had the advantage, because cannons could blast holes in stone walls.

Right: This heavyweight, slow-moving, armoured chariot was drawn by oxen and had long scythes on the sides to ward off enemy horsemen.

Above: This weapon was a cross between a sling and a catapult. The arm was held down with heavy weights at both ends. When the weights were removed, the arm sprang forward and slung a missile over the defenses.

The Alhambra, in Granada, was originally built as a Muslim military fortress, but was transformed into a beautiful palace. It is filled with many peaceful courtyards and gardens.

The Koran, the holy book of Islam, contains the teachings of Muhammad, who received them from a messenger or angel of God.

Islam

Islamic society

Muslim Spain was the most 'civilized' country in Europe. Its culture was much richer and more varied than that of northern Europe. Its people, called 'Moors' by Christians, included Arabs, Berbers from North Africa, Syrians, Jews and native Spaniards. This mixed society was more tolerant than Christian countries and, with some exceptions, Jews and Christians were not persecuted. Many native Spaniards converted to Islam: the Christian bishop of Seville ordered a translation of the Bible into Arabic, as more of his flock knew Arabic than Latin. Many of the best features of Muslim rule, including religious tolerance, disappeared under the later Christian kings.

In 709, Muslims from North Africa landed in Spain. Soon they occupied most of the Spanish peninsula. Muslim Spain gradually broke away from the rest of Islam. In 756, it was conquered by Abd ar-Rahman, a prince of the Umayyad dynasty, and it was ruled as a single empire until the dynasty fell in 1031. Meanwhile, the few tiny Christian kingdoms in the north, supported by the pope, were fighting to regain control of the formerly Christian lands. After 1031, Muslim Spain broke up into smaller kingdoms and was less able to resist the Christian reconquest. By 1300, only the province of Granada was under Muslim rule. It fell in 1492, when Spain became a single, united, Christian kingdom.

Muslims ruled parts of Spain for 500 years, but they were more often politically divided than united.

Medicine

Medicine was more advanced in the Islamic world. It brought together knowledge from ancient Greece and Rome, and showed an understanding of basic chemical processes, such as distillation. Islamic hospitals had separate wards for different diseases. Medical writers such as Ibn Sina (Avicenna) and Ibn Rashd (Averroes) of Cordoba were famous in Christian Europe.

Above: Avicenna (Ibn Sina, 980–1037) was a philosopher and physician who worked at several Islamic courts. Like other Muslim scholars, he tried to bring together Islamic beliefs and the learning of Aristotle and the ancient Greeks.

Above: Muslim scientists were keen on facts and observation, and were less interested in theories. Here, medicines are being made over a fire.

Learning

Muslim knowledge of the sciences was important in medieval Europe not only for its own contributions, but also for its knowledge of other traditions, including that of the ancient Greeks. Works by Aristotle, the greatest Greek thinker, reached Europe through Arabic translations. Christians from many countries came to study under Muslim and Jewish scholars in Spain.

The astrolabe was an instrument that measured the height of the stars above the horizon, allowing navigators to calculate time and position. The finest examples were made in the Islamic world.

Sicily

Sicily was a unique place in the Middle Ages. The Muslims ruled it for about 200 years from the 9th century. It was then conquered by the Normans, and under the Norman king Roger II (1130–54), many cultures blended. Roger's court was the most sophisticated in Europe. He tolerated all races and religions equally, and employed Muslim scholars, including the geographer al-Idirisi, who made a world globe for him out of silver.

This ivory horn was probably made by Muslim craftsmen. It was found in Sicily.

This magnificent bucket, made of bronze with gold and silver decoration, is an example of the beauty of Islamic metalwork. It was made in Afghanistan in 1163.

Right: This scene shows the king of France expelling Jews from his kingdom. Christian kings were generally less tolerant than Islamic rulers.

Industry

Under Muslim rule, Spain prospered in many ways. Irrigation and new crops were introduced, including cotton, sugar cane and rice. Land-ownership was reformed and improved. Many new industries developed, among them pottery, papermaking, sugar-refining and wool and silk-cloth manufacturing. Cordoba alone contained 13,000 weavers. Trade expanded throughout the Mediterranean area, and reached India and central Asia via the Christian merchants of Constantinople.

Islamic craftsmen excelled in ceramics. This 13th-century vase is decorated with scenes from the work of the Persian (Iranian) poet Firdawsi.

Jews

Jews lived in their own communities in towns all over medieval Europe. Their Christian neighbours generally hated them, believing them to be descended from the murderers of Jesus. But many rulers tolerated them for a while, not least because Jews could act as moneylenders, whereas Christians were not supposed to lend money at interest. Moreover, Jews were banned from most other occupations. They were often persecuted, however, and most countries drove them out sooner or later. The Muslim rulers of Spain were more tolerant, and many Jews lived there. But when the last Muslim kingdom fell, the Spanish Christians expelled the Jews.

Crusades

This is a plan of Jerusalem, from a 13th-century map. It shows the Holy City at the centre of the world. Medieval maps were not maps in the modern sense, as knowledge of geography was very limited.

Between the 11th and 14th centuries, the Christians of Europe, urged on by the pope, made a series of expeditions to the Holy Land (Palestine). Their aim was to capture from the Muslims the places sacred to Christianity, above all Jerusalem. Kings, nobles and knights 'took up the Cross', but religious motives were soon overtaken by greed. Many Crusaders wanted to gain land, wealth and fame. One of the motives of the First Crusade was to help the Greek Orthodox Christians of the East oppose their Muslim enemies, but in 1204 the Crusaders themselves captured the Byzantine capital, Constantinople, and for a time took over the Byzantine Empire. Crusades were also launched against the Muslims in Spain (8th–15th centuries) and the Albigensian heretics in southern France (13th century).

The First Crusade

Christian pilgrims had once travelled freely to Jerusalem, but that ended when the powerful Seljuk Turks took over the region. In response, Pope Urban II urged Christians to make the First Crusade. The Crusaders captured Jerusalem, killing its inhabitants, in 1099, and set up small Christian states in Palestine–Syria. But the Crusaders were never as successful again.

Left: Pope Urban II gives his blessing to Crusaders before they embark for the East. He was probably surprised by the eager response to his call for a crusade in 1095.

Christian knights in the later Crusades wore a double head-protector — a metal cap and chain mail underneath a steel helmet. The cross on the helmet marks its wearer as a Crusader.

In old English churches, if a stone figure of a knight on a tomb has his legs crossed, he was a Crusader.

The Third Crusade

The Third Crusade (1189–92) was Europe's response to the fall of Jerusalem to the Muslims. It brought together two great opponents — Saladin and Richard I (the Lionheart), king of England (1189–99), and ended with an honourable truce. After that, Crusaders became more brutal and greedy, with a few exceptions. The last Christian territory, Acre, fell in 1291.

Saladin

Salah al-Din (1138–93), a Kurd by birth, united Egypt and Syria under his rule. In 1187, he defeated the Christian kingdom of Jerusalem and captured Acre. In the Third Crusade, Saladin (as the Christians called him) was defeated by Richard the Lionheart, but Richard could not regain Jerusalem.

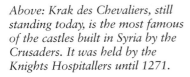

Above: Krak des Chevaliers, still standing today, is the most famous of the castles built in Syria by the Crusaders. It was held by the Knights Hospitallers until 1271.

Right: The Knights Hospitallers owed their name to their original purpose — running a hospital for Christian pilgrims in Jerusalem. They became a warrior order during the Crusades. They still exist as the Knights of Malta.

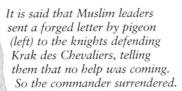

It is said that Muslim leaders sent a forged letter by pigeon (left) to the knights defending Krak des Chevaliers, telling them that no help was coming. So the commander surrendered.

The Children's Crusade

In 1212, about 50,000 children, mainly from France and Germany, were recruited to march on Palestine and recapture it from the Muslims. But none of them ever got that far, and few ever came home. Most of them seem to have been sold as slaves in North Africa. The story of the Pied Piper of Hamelin may be based on this disaster.

Warrior monks

Many of the Crusading knights of Europe were poorly disciplined and disorganized. But the core soldiers were the Knights Templar and the Knights Hospitallers. They were religious orders who took vows like those of monks, except that their religious duty was not to pray but to fight. Their numbers were small, but they were committed warriors, ready to die for Christ.

Saladin receives the king of Jerusalem in his tent after defeating him in battle (1187). In brutal times, Saladin was a gallant opponent. When Richard the Lionheart's horse was killed in battle, Saladin sent him another, saying that so great a warrior should not have to fight on foot.

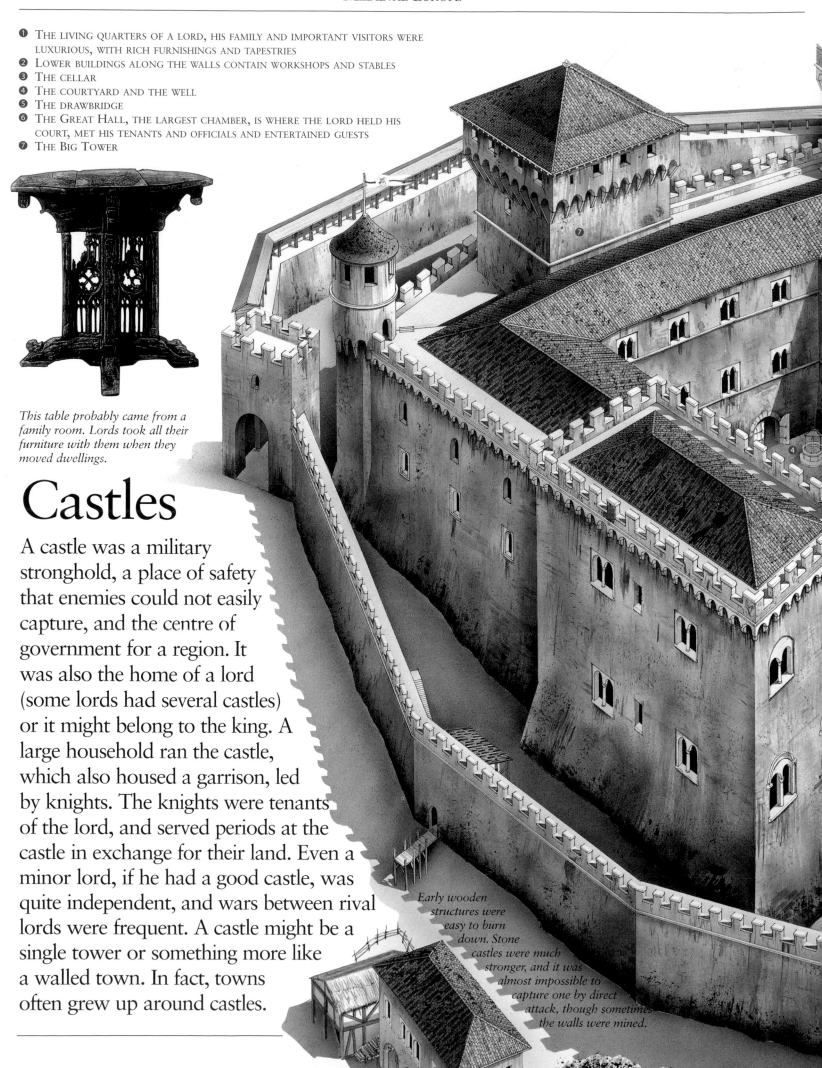

① THE LIVING QUARTERS OF A LORD, HIS FAMILY AND IMPORTANT VISITORS WERE LUXURIOUS, WITH RICH FURNISHINGS AND TAPESTRIES
② LOWER BUILDINGS ALONG THE WALLS CONTAIN WORKSHOPS AND STABLES
③ THE CELLAR
④ THE COURTYARD AND THE WELL
⑤ THE DRAWBRIDGE
⑥ THE GREAT HALL, THE LARGEST CHAMBER, IS WHERE THE LORD HELD HIS COURT, MET HIS TENANTS AND OFFICIALS AND ENTERTAINED GUESTS
⑦ THE BIG TOWER

This table probably came from a family room. Lords took all their furniture with them when they moved dwellings.

Castles

A castle was a military stronghold, a place of safety that enemies could not easily capture, and the centre of government for a region. It was also the home of a lord (some lords had several castles) or it might belong to the king. A large household ran the castle, which also housed a garrison, led by knights. The knights were tenants of the lord, and served periods at the castle in exchange for their land. Even a minor lord, if he had a good castle, was quite independent, and wars between rival lords were frequent. A castle might be a single tower or something more like a walled town. In fact, towns often grew up around castles.

Early wooden structures were easy to burn down. Stone castles were much stronger, and it was almost impossible to capture one by direct attack, though sometimes the walls were mined.

Changing styles

Left: The first castles were wooden 'keeps', built on a mound of earth, protected by a fence. They were linked to other buildings in a bailey (yard).

Right: In the 13th century, castles were larger, more elaborate and built of stone. They often had a double ring of fortified walls, with towers at intervals.

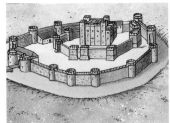

Right: A 14th-century castle with outlying bastions, which made it difficult for attackers to reach the walls. It had no 'keep' — the main buildings were built within the walls.

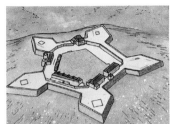

A castle entrance was often guarded by a fortified tower, a drawbridge over the moat, and a portcullis (right) — a heavy wooden grating that could be raised or lowered. Invaders who got past it were trapped in a passage and attacked from above.

Left: This 13th-century castle is guarded by a moat and two sets of fortified walls, one inside the other. The inner wall has battlements and large rounded towers, from which the defenders can fire on enemies attacking any part of the wall. There are no windows large enough for a man to get through. The main tower in the inner court, or bailey, contains living quarters and other rooms, including the chapel. More rooms are in the gatehouse and the towers of the inner walls.

A large flagon from a castle kitchen. It probably contained wine flavoured with herbs.

In the kitchen

Castle cooks had to feed dozens, even hundreds, of people at regular banquets. For one royal visit in 1206, an English castle ordered 1,500 chickens, 20 oxen, 100 pigs and 100 sheep. Meals were cooked over a fire. Fresh meat was usually roasted on spits, and salted meat cooked in huge stew pots. This cook (right) has a pierced spoon and a hook for removing the meat. Few vegetables were served.

Town Life

In the early Middle Ages, most European towns were like large villages. But as the towns and cities grew and prospered, important social changes began to take place. People were able to make money, and this weakened the old social divisions. The landowning lords were challenged by an increasingly rich and powerful new class of merchants and businessmen whose world view was wider than theirs. The merchants led the towns in their struggle for greater independence from the lords, barons and bishops. By about 1300, some cities were independent states. Many gained a charter from the king, giving them rights that prevented the dominance of the local lords. And the king benefited because he gained allies against the powerful nobility.

The first cities to have business centres were in northern Italy, Germany and the Low Countries. As trade and the use of cash increased, merchants needed banking services such as loans and bills of exchange. Bankers (above) were also merchants. In the 1400s, one merchant-banking family, the Medici, became the rulers of Florence.

For centuries, the only large buildings were the castles of the nobility, and the churches and monasteries of the Church. In the 14th century, great buildings like the Palazzo Pubblico (left), the seat of town government in Siena, Italy, proclaimed the rise of the new governing class.

These signs are the trademarks of members of the guild of clothmakers in Florence. Trade was well organized and closely monitored. Guilds controlled markets, weights and measures, and, to some extent, prices.

The ladies of large houses and the stewards of castles carried a bunch of keys at their belt. This lock and key bears the inscription 'IHS' (standing for 'Jesus Christ'). The work shows the locksmith's skill and the importance of religion in all things.

Crafts

Towns were the homes of craftworkers, especially those skilled in the finest crafts, such as goldsmiths, silversmiths and other metalworkers. This carving (right) from a Norwegian church shows an armourer making a sword. One or more streets were often devoted to a single craft, as street names such as Bread Street, Butcher's Row and Tanners Lane remind us. The craftworkers were also shopkeepers. They were helped by journeymen, or day workers, and by apprentice boys learning the trade.

Guilds

Groups of craftworkers, such as goldsmiths, formed associations called guilds to protect trade in their particular crafts. They enforced high standards of work, disliked competition and resisted new methods. Guilds were often religious in character. Members took part in charity work, and some performed religious mystery plays — the main form of medieval theatre. They became an important influence in town life and government.

Markets such as this one, where local goods are being bought and sold, are still held in small towns throughout Europe.

Markets

Some towns grew up around castles or monasteries. Others developed next to rivers or at crossroads, which were good sites for markets. People came to markets from the surrounding countryside to buy and sell food, clothes, tools and whatever they could not make at home. In the early Middle Ages, goods were bartered, or exchanged, for other goods.

People often complained about the state of the streets. Citizens threw garbage, including excrement, out their windows. This created stink and disease. Lucky people drew water from their own wells, but others used public fountains such as this one, or scooped it from the 'dirty' river. Water sellers provided clean water from outside the towns, for a price.

Medieval towns had no police or street lights. Night-watchmen patrolled the towns after dark, carrying a lantern and cudgel (a thick stick).

Law and order

Violence was common in the Middles Ages. Laws were hard to enforce, and justice was rough. People had to look after themselves. Powerful lords lived in stone castles that not even an army could break into. Townspeople depended on city walls, locked doors and support from neighbours. The gates of a city were kept locked at night.

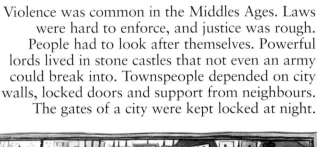

Goods from Asia — mostly luxuries — were bought in small quantities. Spices such as cinnamon (below) were popular.

Most goods from Asia reached Europe via the merchants of Genoa and Venice, and their agents in the Black Sea ports. Pepper (right) came from India. It was used to disguise the unpleasant taste of bad meat.

Trade

Although some old towns are remembered for a particular product (swords from Toledo, for example), the greatest medieval towns owed their importance to their position as centres of trade. They were usually ports, within easy reach of the sea and with good connections inland by road or river. Among the greatest were the Italian ports of Genoa and Venice, which controlled the valuable trade with the East. Equally important were the cities of the Hanseatic League, which dominated trade in northern Europe. There were nearly 100 Hanseatic cities by the 14th century. Rulers often gave privileges to merchants and encouraged trade because it brought them revenue through customs duties. Northern Europe produced goods that the south needed, and vice versa — trade helped to draw Europe together.

The cloth trade

Some silks and cottons were imported from Asia, and flax (used to make linen) was grown in some regions. But most Europeans wore woollen clothes. The finest cloth came from Flanders (Belgium) and Florence (Italy), and was woven with wool from England and Spain. The dyes came from many different places. The finished cloth was sold all over Europe in markets such as this one (below).

Bulky trade goods, such as coal or wine, were transported by boat. Great rivers such as the Rhine and Rhône were very busy. About 1370, the Dutch invented the pound lock, for raising or lowering boats to a different level. This important step encouraged canal-building in many countries during the 14th and 15th centuries.

Transportation

With few proper roads, carts and wagons were unable to travel far, especially in winter. Packhorses did not need roads, however, and were used to carry wool to distant markets, but they were slow. Traders preferred water transportation, as it was cheaper and usually quicker.

Merchants used leather purses for carrying both money and bills of exchange.

The busy port of Lübeck, along with nearby Hamburg, was a founder of the Hanseatic League of merchant cities. The League became almost an independent power.

Money

In the early Middle Ages, money almost disappeared. Trade was by barter — the exchange of goods. But from AD 800, coins reappeared, creating opportunities for moneylenders (often Jews) and, later, bankers. With hundreds of governments issuing their own coins, exchange was often difficult for bankers.

Coins from Venice (below left) and Florence. Medieval coins were not just symbols, like ours are. Their value depended on the amount of gold or silver they contained.

Education

Most people in the Middle Ages did not go to school. Education was practical; children were taught only the skills they needed to live useful lives. Peasant boys learned how to grow crops, look after animals and rebuild houses. Girls were taught to spin, weave and cook. Before the 13th century, few nobles or their wives could read or write. But some nevertheless sent their sons to monastery schools, where they trained to become monks and scholars. Medieval scholars hoped to restore the learning of ancient Greece and Rome. Italy took the lead in non-religious education and had the best universities (founded from the 11th century on). Bologna was a great centre for law, Salerno for medicine.

In the 15th century, cultured Italian princes often owned large libraries. Because books were so valuable, they were often kept locked up with chains.

Books and printing

In an age when all books were written out by hand, they were rare and expensive. In many schools, only the teacher owned a book. The invention of printing in about 1455, and an increase in papermaking, meant that books became cheaper and more widely available. But printing presses were not common until about 1500.

Left: The abbot puts a monk's gown on a novice who has taken his final vows. Monks had tonsures — the crowns of their heads were shaved.

Famous scholars attracted adults to their lectures. Scholarship was international, and there was a kind of brotherhood of scholars, all of whom spoke Latin.

Universities

Clergy dominated the universities as well as the schools (although non-clerical lectures were also given). Famous teachers attracted students from far and wide. Students generally went to university much younger than today, often at 14. They lived in hostels or private homes, sometimes with their master (like an apprentice), or in college halls. In spite of strict rules, it seems medieval students often took part in fights, riots, drunkenness and other bad behaviour.

Religious education

Up to the 12th century, almost the only schools were in monasteries, where the pupils trained to be clergy. (Some schools also accepted the sons of nobles.) Most boys started very young and often never saw their families again. Until the late Middle Ages, they learned to read and write in Latin, the universal language of scholars. At one time, arithmetic was taught using Roman numbers.

Teachers and pupils

Teachers in monastery schools were harsh — even cruel by our standards — toward children. They thought that learning had to be beaten into their pupils. Learning was mostly memorizing.

In the later Middle Ages, the children of nobles often learned their first lessons from their mothers.

Learning a trade

People were expected to remain in the same class that they were born into, so boys usually learned the same trade as their father. At age seven or eight, they were sent to live with another tradesman as his apprentice. The sons of knights and nobles went to live with relatives, who taught them how to ride a horse, hunt and fight.

Right: This boy is learning the trade of coopering (barrel-making) in his father's workshop. Craft skills were often passed from father to son.

Below: Alchemists combined philosophy with experimental science. They believed that they could change one substance into another by changing the balance of its elements: earth, air, fire and water. The greatest alchemist was Paracelsus (b. 1493), being helped here by two young apprentices.

Monasteries

Monasteries, or abbeys, were built to house religious communities of monks or nuns, who made vows to lead simple lives devoted to serving God. The layout tended to follow a similar pattern. The buildings were grouped around the church and its cloisters, and served the various occupations of the community. Monks attended church services several times a day. They farmed the land, cared for the sick, offered hospitality to travellers and produced beautiful 'illuminated' books written out by hand. Most medieval writers and artists were monks. Other monks were skilled craftsmen.

Early Church music was chanted using few notes. It was called plainsong. At first, musical instruments were not allowed. But in time, organs were accepted in churches. Here, a young monk sings to organ music — while a dog joins in!

Books were so rare and valuable that they were chained to library shelves.

Scholarship
The men who served God were the best-educated people in the Middle Ages. They spoke, read and wrote in Latin. Schools were set up in many monasteries.

32

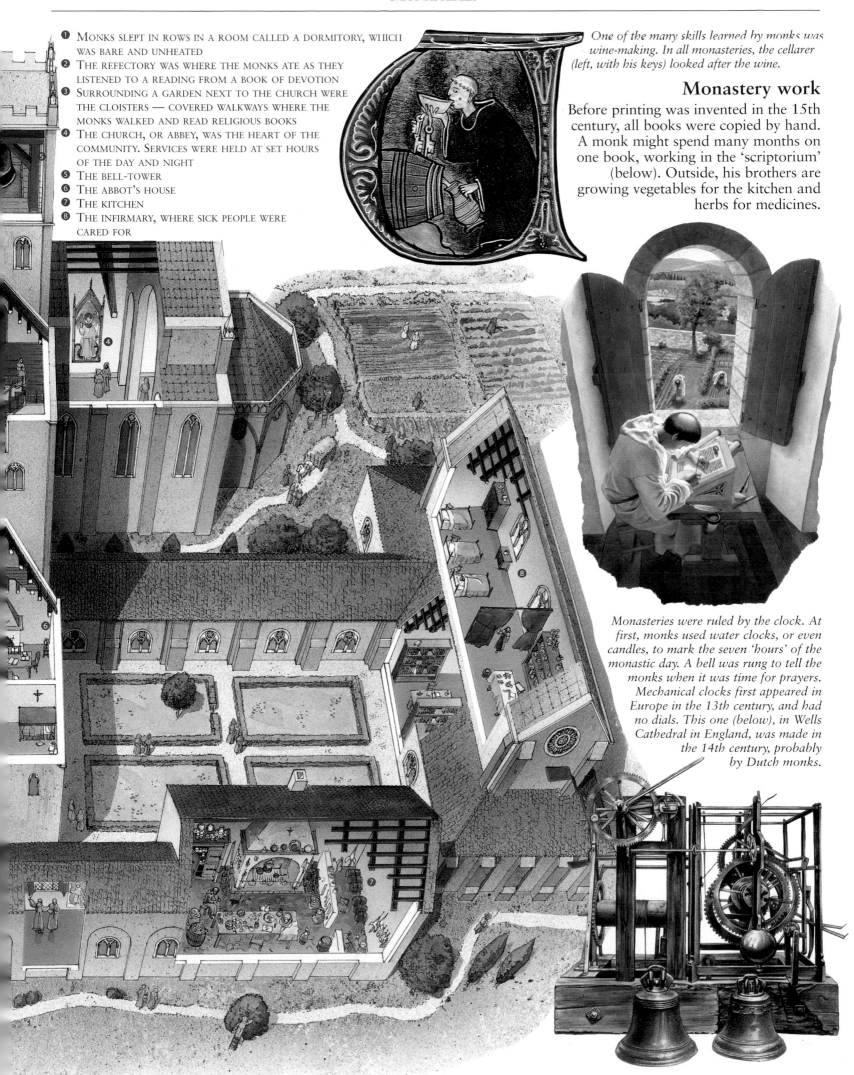

1. MONKS SLEPT IN ROWS IN A ROOM CALLED A DORMITORY, WHICH WAS BARE AND UNHEATED
2. THE REFECTORY WAS WHERE THE MONKS ATE AS THEY LISTENED TO A READING FROM A BOOK OF DEVOTION
3. SURROUNDING A GARDEN NEXT TO THE CHURCH WERE THE CLOISTERS — COVERED WALKWAYS WHERE THE MONKS WALKED AND READ RELIGIOUS BOOKS
4. THE CHURCH, OR ABBEY, WAS THE HEART OF THE COMMUNITY. SERVICES WERE HELD AT SET HOURS OF THE DAY AND NIGHT
5. THE BELL-TOWER
6. THE ABBOT'S HOUSE
7. THE KITCHEN
8. THE INFIRMARY, WHERE SICK PEOPLE WERE CARED FOR

One of the many skills learned by monks was wine-making. In all monasteries, the cellarer (left, with his keys) looked after the wine.

Monastery work

Before printing was invented in the 15th century, all books were copied by hand. A monk might spend many months on one book, working in the 'scriptorium' (below). Outside, his brothers are growing vegetables for the kitchen and herbs for medicines.

Monasteries were ruled by the clock. At first, monks used water clocks, or even candles, to mark the seven 'hours' of the monastic day. A bell was rung to tell the monks when it was time for prayers. Mechanical clocks first appeared in Europe in the 13th century, and had no dials. This one (below), in Wells Cathedral in England, was made in the 14th century, probably by Dutch monks.

Health and Medicine

In the Middle Ages, people died of simple illnesses and infections that are easily cured today. The average lifetime was less than 40 years, and the death rate among small children was very high. Medicine was very different — it had nothing to do with chemistry or biology, and was based on a mixture of folklore, religious beliefs and a little of the medical knowledge of the ancient Greeks, which reached Europe through the work of Islamic scholars. One book of cures recommended medicines based on herbs, but it also recommended magic spells and charms. Some people believed that the stars influenced health, others that illness was God's punishment. Most 'cures' did more harm than good.

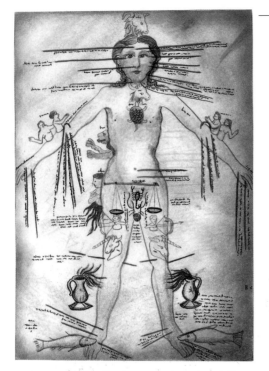

The signs of the zodiac were linked to different parts of the body. Many physicians prescribed treatments according to the position of the stars, rather than the patient's symptoms.

Hygiene

Ordinary people did not understand the dangers of infection and had no knowledge of germs. In towns, toilets emptied into open drains, and wells became polluted. Disease spread quickly as a result. People threw pails of rotten food and household waste into the streets. Street cleaners were employed, but they did little more than clear a way so carts could pass by. People often shared their homes with farm animals. They covered the bare earthen floors of their cottages with rushes or straw, which lay filthy and rotting, providing a breeding place for germs. People were used to the dreadful smells.

Plague was carried by fleas that lived on black rats. The rats reached Europe on trading ships from Asia, where plague had already killed huge numbers of people. When the fleas from the rats infested people's homes, the epidemic began. Plague continued to strike Europe at intervals, on a smaller scale, until the late 17th century. It seems to have stopped when black rats were replaced by the brown rats that live in Europe today. Brown rats do not carry the plague-bearing fleas.

Above: This house has the convenience of an outdoor toilet — a rough seat above a hole in the ground.

The Black Death

The plague epidemic that swept Europe in 1348–49 was the worst human disaster in European history. More than one quarter of the population died. Whole villages were wiped out. When it returned in later years, it helped to cause a crisis of economic decline, violence and low population that lasted more than a century. The Black Death, as it was known, was made up of three different types of plague, including bubonic plague, which was the most infectious. From this time, however, medical knowledge began to advance, especially in Italian universities.

Doctors wore a costume that shows they were aware of the dangers of infection. This suit covered every part of the doctor and even had flaps to cover the eyes. The 'beak' contained strong-smelling herbs, which he hoped would 'clean' the air that he breathed.

During the Black Death, bodies were buried in mass graves, often without coffins. Sometimes not enough people survived an outbreak to bury the dead, and bodies were left to rot.

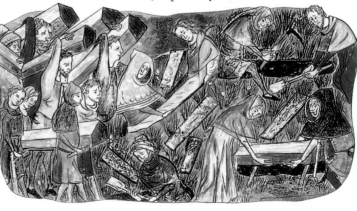

Surgeons and doctors

With no anesthetics, surgery was extremely painful, and if patients survived an operation, they were likely to die from an infection afterwards. Surgeons also practised as barbers! Physicians (doctors) had a higher status in society. But they had a reputation for being more interested in their fee than in their patients. Blood-letting — the removal of blood — was a common cure, but was often worse than the illness.

In this 13th-century illustration from Salerno, Italy — the first European centre of medical knowledge — a surgeon prepares to remove a spear and arrow from a man's chest.

Herbs and medicines

Apothecaries made up medicines from natural ingredients. Monasteries often had a large herb garden, and grew spices and medicinal plants. Without doubt, some worked. Mandrake (left) contains a chemical that affects the nerves, and was used in many cures.

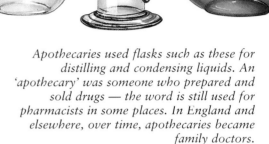

Apothecaries used flasks such as these for distilling and condensing liquids. An 'apothecary' was someone who prepared and sold drugs — the word is still used for pharmacists in some places. In England and elsewhere, over time, apothecaries became family doctors.

Hospitals

Hospital care was provided by monks and nuns, who looked after the sick in special wards in monasteries. They cared mainly for the poor, who had no one else to look after them, and for travellers or victims of disaster. Ordinary doctors and surgeons did not attend these hospitals. From the 14th century, non-monastic hospitals were founded in cities such as Florence, Italy. They were charities, funded by rich citizens, guilds and religious organizations.

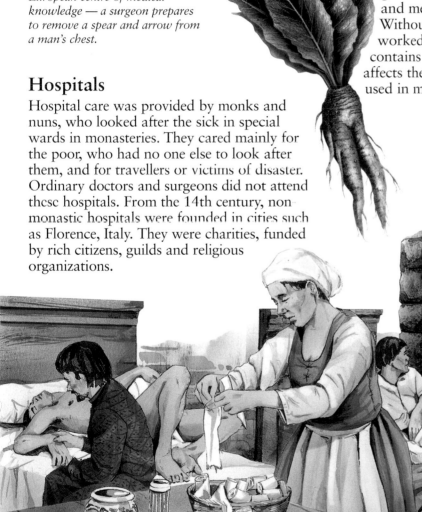

Women

The ladies of medieval courts were often entertained by long narrative poems called 'romances', in which knights were inspired to do great deeds so that they would be worthy of their lady's love. In the 'courtly love' relationship, women played an active and important role, which did not correspond to real life.

In medieval society, men were considered superior to women. A woman's duty in life was to be a wife, housekeeper and mother. A man was legally entitled to beat his wife if she 'misbehaved'. The reality was often different. We hear of women who had a trade or worked with their husbands. Family letters tell of marriages that were loving partnerships. Yet women did suffer severe handicaps. The Church, which regarded sex as sinful except for producing children, was anti-women. It saw women as agents of the devil, tempting men into sin. Yet the upper-class ideal of 'courtly love' painted women as models of virtue.

Nuns

Convents, or nunneries, housed communities of women belonging to a religious order who took the same kind of vows as monks. Their members came from the higher classes — this nun (right) is Marie de Bourbon, sister of the queen of France. For such women, entering a convent was the only alternative to marriage. Some nunneries were very poor, but nuns, like monks, often bent the strict rules of the order and lived fairly comfortable lives.

Marriage

Girls got married as young as age 11 or 12. Few married for love — though it often developed later. Among the nobility, a child's future husband or wife was chosen by the parents or guardians, with the aim of increasing the family's property. Among serfs, marriages were arranged by the overlord. (In the early Middle Ages, serfs were often not married in church.) The Church did not accept divorce, though occasionally marriages were annulled. A wife's property belonged to her husband.

Widows

Women often married older men, and they tended to live longer, so many became widows. As widows, they were entitled to inherit part of their husbands' estates (as well as being able to own property in their own right). Some remained as head of the household after their husbands had died. But a rich widow could usually find another husband if she wanted. Or she might become a nun.

Motherhood

Most married couples tried to produce lots of children because only about one in four survived early childhood. Children had a great variety of toys, but childhood was short, even for those who lived. From age seven, most children started work or began to train in a craft. Boys generally left home; girls stayed home longer, learning domestic skills and crafts from their mothers.

Above: The girl-warrior Joan of Arc is probably the best-known woman from medieval times. Here she is shown presenting documents to the king.

Working women

Women, even those with servants, had plenty of work to do running a household and supervising the children. Besides cooking and cleaning, a woman had to spin yarn from wool and weave it into cloth, which she made into clothes. The distaff, a stick for holding yarn, became a symbol for the female gender. In towns, women worked as skilled craftworkers, shopkeepers and merchants.

Among serfs and peasants, wives and husbands sometimes worked side by side.

Learned women

Few people wrote plays in the Middle Ages. The best-known playwright was a German nun named Hroswitha, who lived in the 10th century. By about 1300, some women of the higher classes could read and write, often in Latin and French (which is derived from Latin). Noble French ladies wrote love songs. After her husband's death, Christine de Pisan made a living as a professional writer, something that was extremely rare in the days before printing existed in Europe.

Christine de Pisan (died 1429) wrote several books defending the rights of women.

Sports and Games

Most medieval sports were violent, and were a way of training for war. Boys were supposed to practise archery, not play football. The favourite sports of kings and nobles were hunting and jousting (fighting mock duels). Ordinary people enjoyed sports that we consider cruel, such as cockfights and bear-baiting (setting dogs to attack a chained bear). They also played games — probably the early forms of modern ones — such as hockey and football. A whole village sometimes took part in a football match that might cover several miles. There were no rules and no referee, and the game often turned into a riot. Governments passed laws to prevent its play.

These children are sitting on the shoulders of adults, trying to knock each other off their perches.

Children

Young children played games with hoops, tops, marbles and dolls, as many still do today. They even built sandcastles on the beach. Adults encouraged boys to play 'fighting' games, such as boxing and wrestling.

Tournaments

The main attraction of these colourful entertainments was jousting (above), in which knights tried to knock each other from their horses with blunted lances. Tournaments were especially popular during the 'age of chivalry', when knights were supposed to keep high standards of honour and gallantry. But it was a dangerous sport. A king of France was killed when a splinter entered his eye and pierced his brain.

Board games

Games with counters or dice were popular, including some that were similar to backgammon or checkers. Chess arrived in Europe, probably brought by Arab traders, in the 11th century. It was good training for tactics in battle. Playing cards were unknown until the 15th century. Although people worked long hours and had no long annual vacations, there were many saints' days throughout the year, when people were not supposed to work.

Above: These Norwegian chesspieces, carved from walrus tusks, were made in the 12th century.

Although the Church taught that gambling was a sin, it was as popular in the Middle Ages as at any other time. These men (above) are gambling with dice. People also bet on cockfights and other animal contests.

Left: Many games were played with a stick and a ball, but we do not know what the rules were. Usually the only evidence is a few pictures such as this one.

Huntsmen generally chased and killed deer and wild boar, although other animals were hunted too. Professional huntsmen, wearing livery (uniform), were employed on rich estates. Hunting dogs were similar to today's greyhounds and mastiffs.

Ball games

People were playing ball games before history began. Some may have been connected with ancient religious beliefs, though Homer described girls playing catch for fun in the 8th century BC. In medieval games, golf or boule balls were made of wood, footballs from an animal's stomach or bladder and tennis balls from leather stuffed with cloth. Monks played the original form of tennis — called 'real' tennis — which is still played in a few special courts today.

Hunting

By the 14th century, people viewed hunting as a sport and not just a way to obtain meat. In well-populated countries such as England, most of the countryside that was not farmed was reserved for hunting by its owners. Ordinary people were banned from hunting, but were allowed to trap small animals. Fishing was not a respected sport because it depended on guile rather than aggression.

Right: Falconry (hunting with trained hawks or falcons) was almost as popular with nobles and knights as stag-hunting. The sport began in Asia and reached Europe in about the 10th century. It was the easiest way to catch birds such as ducks or pigeons.

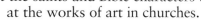

The Gothic style

Early medieval architecture was described as 'Romanesque', meaning 'like the style of ancient Rome' — massive and solid. Gradually, masons learned to build thinner walls, higher roofs, and — in northern Europe, where light was less bright — huge windows. These new techniques led to the 'Gothic' style of architecture, characterized by pointed arches, 'flying' buttresses, walls with more glass than stone and dizzily high vaulted ceilings and spires. Strasbourg's spire, which was the tallest, rose to 480 feet (146 m).

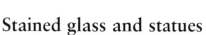

Medieval glass is now rare. The 13th-century windows of Chartres Cathedral, which glow intensely blue and red when lit from behind, are unique. The illustrations present religious stories in jewel-like colours.

Medieval people were fascinated by weird monsters. This gargoyle (a decorative gutter spout) watches over Paris from the roof of Notre Dame Cathedral.

Stained glass and statues

Nearly all medieval art was religious, and churches were like art galleries. They were decorated with stone sculptures and pictorial windows in stained glass, and were painted from floor to ceiling with religious scenes and decorations (most of the wall-paintings have now disappeared). People were able to learn about the saints and Bible characters by looking at the works of art in churches.

The teacher and monk Ekkehart (above left) and abbess Uta (above right) were founders of Naumburg Cathedral (c. 1249). Their sculptures stand in the west choir of the cathedral.

❶ WEST DOOR
❷ BELL TOWER
❸ THE NAVE, WHERE PEOPLE STOOD OR WALKED ABOUT DURING SERVICES
❹ THICK STONE PILLARS SUPPORTED THE VAULTED ROOF AND SEPARATED THE NAVE FROM THE SIDE AISLES

Cathedrals

A cathedral is simply a Christian church that contains the seat, or throne (*cathedra* in Latin), of a bishop. Most western cathedrals are built in the shape of a cross. The long part, called the nave, runs east-west, and is crossed by two transepts to the north and south. The great cathedrals were the finest buildings of medieval Europe, and remind us of the huge importance of the Christian religion in people's lives during the Middle Ages. They were so large, intricate and expensive that they took at least 100 years to build (most took far longer). Bishops were senior members of the Christian Church, in charge of dioceses, or districts. Higher in rank were the archbishops, who were as rich and powerful as princes. Archbishops answered to the overall head of the Church — God's representative on Earth — the pope.

❺ CHOIR STALLS IN THE CHANCEL, THE PART OF THE CATHEDRAL RESERVED FOR THE CLERGY AND CHOIR. HOLY COMMUNION WAS HELD HERE AT THE ALTAR
❻ FLYING BUTTRESSES SUPPORT THE STRUCTURE, ALLOWING WALLS TO BE THINNER AND WINDOWS LARGER

The 'Angel Pillar' stands in the south transept of Strasbourg Cathedral, where the bishop held his court and 'mystery plays' were performed by the guilds. Mystery plays were spoken in verse and had religious subjects.

Carpenters built the huge scaffolding needed to erect a cathedral. So much wood was needed that often one piece of scaffolding had to be taken down and reused elsewhere on the same building. A hoist, powered by a treadmill (right), was used to raise stone to the tops of walls.

The builders

The building plans of Europe's great cathedrals were created by gifted priests or monks, such as Abbot Suger of St. Denis, pioneer of the Gothic style. But the names of the carpenters and masons who actually built the cathedrals, carved the sculpture and made the windows and furnishings are unknown. Masons were professional craftsmen, and master masons were architects in all but name. United in guilds, masons moved from one site to another, enjoying an unusual degree of independence for the time.

Travel

Many people in the Middle Ages lived their whole lives within a mile or two of their birthplace. Serfs were not allowed to move away — they were bound to the land or their landlord. Most people knew nothing about other countries and believed all sorts of strange stories about them, including tales of giants and monsters. But some people did make journeys and occasionally very long ones. Merchants regularly visited foreign countries. Soldiers and Crusaders travelled to distant wars. Pilgrims from all over Europe journeyed to Rome, Constantinople and Jerusalem. Entertainers toured the great fairs. Ambassadors attended foreign courts as far away as China, and kings made visits to all their estates, sometimes in other countries.

A Venetian named Marco Polo was the most famous European traveller in the Middle Ages. He went to China and spent more than 20 years there. Many people did not believe his stories about a civilization much more advanced than Europe. This picture (left) comes from Polo's Wonders of the World, *which reported fantastic creatures such as humans with no heads, and faces on their chests.*

The chief shrine for English pilgrims was in Canterbury Cathedral, where Archbishop Becket died a martyr in 1170. The Canterbury Tales (right) were written by the poet Chaucer some 200 years later. The tales — some funny, some bawdy, some exciting — are told by a group of pilgrims on their way to Canterbury.

A knowledge of geography was more advanced in the Islamic world. This map is by al-Idirisi (c. 1099–1165), who was born in Spain and later travelled widely before working for Roger II of Sicily. On this map the south is at the top. Turn it upside-down and you can see the Mediterranean, the Red Sea, the Persian Gulf leading to the Indian Ocean and the Nile River in Egypt.

Pilgrims

Both Christians and Muslims made long journeys to visit holy places, or shrines. The most popular was the cathedral at Compostela in northwestern Spain, said to be the burial place of St. James, one of Jesus's Twelve Apostles. The route to Compostela was largely organized by the French abbey of Cluny. Other monasteries along the way provided food and shelter.

Geography

Medieval Europeans had little idea of the world, which they thought was flat. Although their ships crossed seas such as the Mediterranean and the Baltic, they did not venture out into the oceans. Countries such as India and China were places of fantasy, just like the distant stars are in science-fiction stories today. Africa was unknown beyond its northern coasts, and the Americas and Australasia had not been discovered. Medieval maps show one continent with Jerusalem at the centre.

Left: This illustration comes from a 12th-century French guide for pilgrims heading for remote Compostela. It gives advice on things such as the quality of the water along the route, and criticizes the greedy ferrymen who profited from the pilgrims.

In the early Middle Ages, there were no country inns along main routes. But as travel increased, inns and taverns appeared in the growing towns. The food was usually simple, and people had to share beds. As well as food and shelter, inns offered safety and company to travellers. Although they may have been more enjoyable than the charity of monasteries, they were also more expensive.

Roads and bridges

The best roads in Europe were those that the Romans had built centuries before. But an increase in traffic, especially carts with studded wheels, began to wear them out, and there was no emperor to ensure they were kept in good order. Local roads and bridges were built by lords or rich men as an act of charity, and travellers had to pay a toll toward the cost of maintenance. Large areas had no proper roads at all.

Above: In the late Middle Ages, fine stone bridges, such as the 13th-century 'Devil's Bridge', were built in prosperous northern Italy. But bridges such as this were uncommon in Europe.

Right: With roads unfit for carriages, a French princess — on her way to marry an English king in the 14th century — makes her arrival in a pavilion on shafts, carried by horses.

Royal courts

Kings and rulers were often on the move. In an age with no news media, a king needed to show himself in all parts of his kingdom from time to time, to support his local officials and remind people who the ruler was. A king did not travel alone. His household and sometimes his court moved with him. When no permanent seat of government existed, the government itself moved with the king. A ruler of many lands had to be a vigorous traveller. In just one month in 1172, King Henry II of England travelled from Ireland to England and then to France — a journey of about 800 miles (1,300 km), with two sea crossings.

Right: Pilgrims usually travelled on foot. They stayed in groups, for fear of being attacked by thieves.

Merchants preferred to travel by river if possible. If they had to make a sea voyage, they made their wills first.

Travelling

The fastest method of overland travel for individuals was on horseback. Merchants moved their goods on mules or packhorses. The longest journey that European merchants made overland was to China. They travelled in a caravan along the Silk Road through central Asia. The route was open only for a short time in the 13th century, and was taken by Marco Polo.

Clothes and the Cloth Business

After food, people's greatest need is clothing, which is why the wool industry and the cloth trade were the biggest economic activities in medieval Europe after farming and food. Peasants — the largest sector of society — wore simple clothes that did not change in style. The basic garment was a smock or long shirt, gathered at the waist. The cloth was often made from wool shorn from the family's sheep, and spun and woven into cloth at home. For richer people, clothes were more complicated, and in the 14th and 15th centuries fashions changed quite fast. But certain rules applied. Skirts were never shorter than ankle-length, although necklines could be quite low. Usually women's hair was covered, too. Men could show off their legs in hose (stockings) and short jackets.

This 13th-century nobleman from Florence is wearing a padded tunic with his armour. For most of the period, men and women wore fitted tunics.

This woman (below) is 'carding' or combing the wool from a sheep's fleece using a toothed instrument. Carding untangled the fibres so the wool could be spun.

Women of all classes spun and wove cloth at home. The lady in the red dress is spinning yarn from wool that has been carded (combed). She is using a stick called a distaff, which was later replaced by the spinning wheel. Other mechanical improvements in cloth-making were introduced in the 13th to 15th centuries. The lady in green is weaving cloth on a loom.

Above: An Italian city dignitary displays his coat of squirrel fur. It was a sign of his status as an important official.

The cloth industry

A great many different crafts were involved in cloth-making — spinning, weaving and dyeing, for example. Each craft had its own guild. Most workshops were small. A typical cloth-maker ran a shop with five or six assistants. By the 15th century, a few large workshops existed, with ten or more looms. Florence, in about 1325, was producing 100,000 pieces of cloth a year, while the industry supported no less than 30,000 people.

Above: These men are dyers. They belonged to their own guild and usually worked freelance for cloth-makers. Sometimes the wool fleece was dyed, sometimes the yarn, and sometimes the finished cloth.

Right: This angel is a small detail from the seven enormous tapestries that together make up the 'Angers Apocalypse'. One of the most famous of all medieval tapestries, it was made in Angers in the 14th century.

Tapestries

Tapestries were made in the late Middle Ages, for warmth and for decoration. They were woven on looms using wool or the costliest silks. Weavers followed a detailed design called a 'cartoon' for the shapes and colours. Towns in Flanders (Belgium) and northern France were the main tapestry centres. An 'arras' (after the town of the same name) became another word for a tapestry.

Fancy fabrics

Wool was the most common cloth, ranging from rough homespun to super-fine worsted, like that being fitted in an Italian tailor's shop (above). Linen, made from flax, replaced wool in some regions. Some cottons and silks were imported, and later were produced in southern Italy. Hemp, chiefly for canvas and rope, came from the Balkans (southeastern Europe), where furs were also made. An ermine-trimmed coat was a sign of great distinction.

Right: This magnificent mantle (for covering the shoulders) was made by Muslim craftsmen in Sicily for the coronation of Roger II in 1130. It was later worn by the Holy Roman emperors.

Left: A high-class 15th-century lady admires her pale complexion and expensive dress in a mirror. She is wearing the fashionable cone-shaped headdress called a 'hennin', with a veil trailing from the tip.

Sumptuary laws

Everyone had to dress according to their place in society. A priest was not supposed to dress like a layman, nor a woman from a merchant family like a noblewoman. The sumptuary laws tried to enforce this. (Today we might call them laws against 'conscious consumption'.) But they were widely broken. As merchants grew wealthier, their families wore more and more expensive clothes.

Footwear

Peasants wore homemade clogs or went barefoot. Some wore thick soles of wood or cork to keep their feet out of the mud. It was also possible to buy hose (stockings) with wooden soles attached (shoes with heels came along in later centuries). The finest shoe leather came from Cordoba in Spain — origin of the word 'cordwainer', or 'cobbler' (shoemaker).

Below: Soft, impractical shoes with long toes were in fashion during the 13th to 15th centuries. Laws dictated maximum toe-lengths, but the tips of some shoes were so long that they had to be tied around the leg below the knee with a chain!

Index